a very short, entirely true

HISTORY *of* UNICORNS

by SARAH LASKOW
illustrated by SAM BECK

Penguin Workshop

the *IDEAL* UNICORN

IMAGINE A unicorn. Most likely, your unicorn is white with a flowing mane and a spiraling horn pointing from its forehead. It looks more or less like a horse. Perhaps its hair is streaked with bright colors, or a rainbow is streaming across the sky behind it.

Your unicorn probably doesn't have a tail curled like a wild pig's or a beard like a goat's. It's probably not fighting an elephant. It probably doesn't live along the border of the United States and Canada.

But those are all actual ideas that people have had about unicorns at one time or another.

If you searched the whole world, it would be impossible to find a magical one-horned horse. Unicorns, as we imagine them now, aren't real. But show anyone a picture of a unicorn, and they'll know exactly what it is.

People have been talking and thinking about unicorns for thousands of years.

This is the very real history of why we once believed these mythical creatures existed, and how they evolved into the beloved, majestic fantasy animals of today.

WHO WOULD BELIEVE
in a HORSE *with a* HORN?

CTESIAS

MORE THAN 2,300 years ago, there was a Greek doctor who lived in Persia named Ctesias (say: TEE-zee-yus). Actually, he was a little bit obsessed with Persia, the empire most closely associated with modern-day Iran. He spent almost two decades there and eventually wrote a very long history—twenty-three books in all—just about Persia.

To the east of the Persian Empire was India, which Ctesias knew less about. Still, he managed to write an entire book about this faraway place, too, in which he reported the existence of fantastic one-horned "wild asses." (*Ass* is another word for donkey and is defined as "a hoofed mammal of the horse family with a braying call.")

Ctesias had a pretty clear idea of what these wild creatures looked like. "Their bodies are white, their heads dark red, and their eyes dark blue," he wrote. "They have one horn on the forehead which is about a foot and a half in length."

That horn, according to Ctesias, was pure white at the bottom, black in the middle, and crimson red at its tip. This animal was "exceedingly swift and powerful," and it was fierce. No other creature could outrun it, and it could not be caught alive.

Ctesias had never seen the wild ass with a horn. But he wrote about other imaginary animals in his book, too. These included the manticore, which has a human face and a lion's body, and a monkey with a six-foot-long tail. He also described the elephant, which was unknown in Europe at the time but very real in Persia. So for Ctesias, unicorns were as real as elephants.

the UNICORN EVOLVES

AFTER CTESIAS, other Greek and Roman writers kept describing a swift, one-horned animal as if it were real. Many of their accounts were based on Ctesias's original description. But every writer added slightly different details.

A unicorn described in the first century AD had the body of a horse, the head of a stag, the feet of an elephant, the tail of a boar, and a three-foot-long black horn.

Two hundred years later, the unicorn had a reddish coat, and its horn was described as being four feet long and spiral.

A book called *Physiologus* had a different idea. It said the unicorn was small, like a goat.

A Greek traveler named Cosmas Indicopleustes wrote that unicorns used their horns to break their fall when they jumped off cliffs.

By the 1200s, some writers thought the unicorn's horn was ten feet long!

A few hundred years after that, one traveler had shrunk the unicorn's horn back to three feet—but this unicorn had webbed feet and lived on fish.

They didn't use the word *unicorn*, but still, these writers all thought they were talking about the same one-horned animal. Some qualities appeared in every description: The unicorn was fierce, it was shy, and it was hard to catch.

ONE HORN, MANY NAMES

DIFFERENT LANGUAGES have different words for unicorns. But usually they follow a simple formula. They combine the word for *one* or *only* with the word for *horn*.

In Latin, *unus* means "one," and *cornu* means "horn." That's where the word *unicorn* comes from. Across Europe, languages related to Latin use similar words. An Italian unicorn is a *unicorno*, a Spanish unicorn is a *unicornio*, and a French unicorn is a *licorne*.

In Greek, *monos* means "only" or "single," and *keras* means "horn."
A unicorn is a *monoceros*.

German follows the same formula. *Ein* (one) + *horn* (horn) = *Einhorn*. The Dutch
speak of the *eenhoorn*. In Old Norse, a unicorn is *einhyrningr*, so Norwegians say
enhjørning, and Icelanders say *einhyrningur*.

PICS *or*
it DIDN'T HAPPEN

THE GREEK traveler Cosmas Indicopleustes drew one of the first pictures of a unicorn around the year 545. He had been traveling in a place he called Ethiopia, a large area located near India (not the modern African country of Ethiopia). His image, he wrote, was inspired by four bronze figures he saw at the palace of an emperor he met on his journey.

The original illustration disappeared long ago. But when other people made copies of Cosmas Indicopleustes's travel journal, they also copied his drawing. The oldest copy that still exists is in a manuscript from about a thousand years ago.

This isn't even the earliest piece of art to represent a unicorn, though. One of the earliest images of a one-horned creature is a sculpture from about 2,800 years ago. It's a small bronze statue that was made in Persia of a four-legged, horse-like creature with a large horn sprouting from its forehead. It looks a lot like a unicorn! And it may be the sort of statue that inspired Cosmas Indicopleustes's drawing.

The earliest unicorn image

INTERNATIONAL
UNICORNS

HUMANS AROUND the world, not just Europeans, have been telling stories about unicorn-like creatures for thousands of years.

QILIN

This mythical Chinese creature has the body of a deer, the long and ropy tail of an ox, and the same hooves as a horse. Sometimes it has two horns, but often only one, which can be twelve feet long. The *qilin* (say: TCHI-lin) is red, yellow, blue, black, and white, and it has great respect for living things. It doesn't eat meat, and it tries not to crush insects or grass when it walks.

In Chinese tradition, the *qilin* can tell the future and is sometimes a sign that a great man will soon die. According to legend, the famous scholar Confucius saw a *qilin* not long before he died and was one of the last people ever to see the magical being.

CAMAHUETO

In the south of Chile, there is a myth about a bull-like creature with a single horn on its forehead. A *camahueto* is born from a piece of horn buried in the hills. And when it's fully grown, it destroys everything in its way as it runs to its adult home, in the sea.

XAR Ī SE PĀY (THREE-LEGGED ASS)

Zoroastrian ideas from Persia about how the universe began include a mythical creature that's as big as a mountain, with a white body and a dark blue head. It has two ears, three feet, six eyes, and one hollow golden horn.

the STORY of
RISHYASRINGA

INDIA HAS a story about a different kind of one-horned animal—a unicorn-like man. In two ancient epic poems written in the language Sanskrit, there's a character named Rishyasringa, who was born with a horn on his head. His father was a religious person who ate and drank as little as possible, and his mother was a deer.

Rishyasringa's father raised him in the woods, where he encountered very few human beings. But one day a king sent a woman from his court to find the one-horned man. There was a drought and the king believed Rishyasringa could bring the rain back.

When the woman reached the forest, she convinced Rishyasringa to follow her onto a boat. Immediately, she took him back to the king.

Once Rishyasringa arrived, rain returned to the kingdom. The king's own daughter agreed to marry the one-horned man. Rishyasringa's father was upset to find his son gone. But when he discovered that Rishyasringa had become a wealthy and respected man, he accepted that it had all been for the best.

The epic Sanskrit poems *Ramayana* and *Mahabharata* are long stories about Indian heroes and gods.

a MAP of UNICORNS, NEAR and FAR

As European travelers journeyed farther from home, they reported the existence of unicorns in places all around the world.

Tibet (1224)
Palestine (1389)
Mecca (1503)
Florida (1564)
Mountains of the Moon (1573)
Carpathian Mountains (1500s)
The Cape of Good Hope (1600s)

Scandinavia (1628)
The Bronx (1673)
The Canadian border (1673)
The Red River of Louisiana (1719)
Caucasus Mountains (1700s)
Congo (1861)

But they always had secondhand information. None of them had actually *seen* a unicorn.

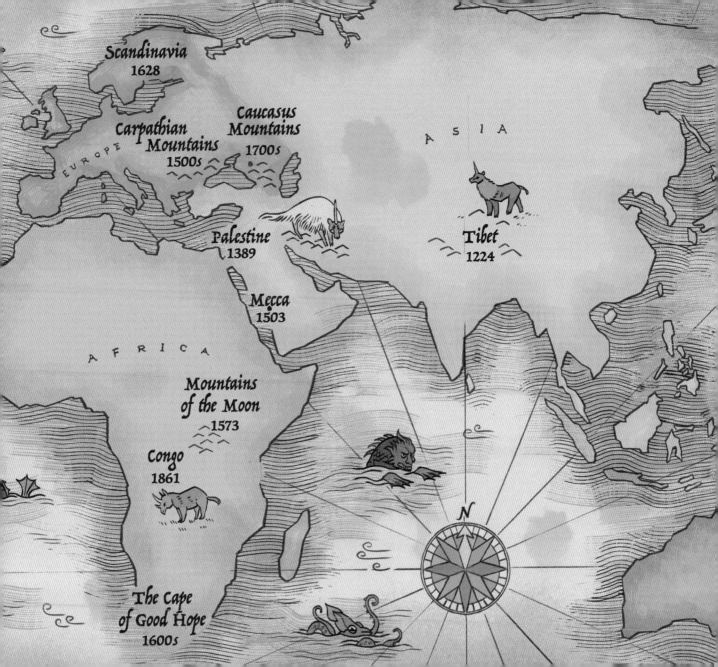

Scandinavia
1628

Carpathian
Mountains
1500s

Caucasus
Mountains
1700s

EUROPE

ASIA

Palestine
1389

Tibet
1224

Mecca
1503

AFRICA

Mountains
of the Moon
1573

Congo
1861

N

The Cape
of Good Hope
1600s

WHY *are there* UNICORNS *in the* BIBLE?

THE BIBLE mentions unicorns many times. But Hebrew Bibles (the original text) use the word *re'em*. Today, unicorn scholars believe that a *re'em* wasn't a one-horned animal at all.

The problem may have started with the seventy-two scribes who were hired by the king of Egypt to translate the Hebrew Bible into Greek. According to legend, they all had to work alone, so that they wouldn't influence each other's work. But even so, they all came up with the exact same translation!

Whoever made the earliest known Greek translation of the Bible didn't know what a *re'em* was. The animal is never described as having only one horn. But the translators knew a *re'em* was strong, powerful, and mysterious. Scholars believe it's possible a translator had read about the unicorn in Ctesias's book and decided the *re'em* was the same creature.

Many years later, a zoologist solved the mystery of the *re'em*. He knew of a similar word, *rimu*, written in ancient cuneiform, a kind of writing used thousands of years ago, and he realized that a *rimu* and a *re'em* just might be the same creature.

He also figured out the identity of the *rimu*. It was a large animal, now extinct, called an aurochs. The aurochs is the ancestor of a very common animal, the cow, so it's safe to say the *re'em* of the Bible would have been more like a powerful, giant ox than a unicorn.

REAL-LIFE UNICORNS

UNICORN SCHOLARS have tried to figure out what other real-life animals may have inspired unicorn descriptions and reports of unicorn sightings.

INDIAN RHINOCEROS

The most obvious choice is the rhinoceros. It lives in India, where reports of unicorns originated, and it has a single horn.

Rhinoceros horns are made of keratin, just like fingernails and hooves. They are usually one or two feet long and can weigh up to six pounds.

CHIRU

Smaller than a horse, this Tibetan antelope has two long, narrow, pointy horns growing from its forehead. But from the side, a chiru can look like it has just one horn. It lives high in the mountains that border northern India, so it could have inspired the original rumors Ctesias heard.

There are many types of horned antelopes, so the chiru is just one possible unicorn explanation. The oryx, like the chiru, also has long, thin horns.

OKAPI

Okapis live in central Africa and look a bit like a few different animals pasted together. They have striped legs like a zebra, a body like a horse, and a head like a giraffe. They actually *are* related to the giraffe, and like giraffes, they have horn-like structures on their heads called *ossicones* (say: OSS-eh-cones). They're very rare creatures, and they may be the source of unicorn rumors in Africa.

UNICORNFISH

This type of fish has a "rostral protuberance"—a fancy way of saying "something sticking out of its face"—that makes it look like a unicorn. Different unicornfish can have different-size horns. They live around coral reefs in the Pacific and Indian Oceans, and when they're young, they eat algae from the coral.

But when some unicornfish get older, their growing horns keep them from reaching the algae. They have to change their whole diet to survive. Their horns prevent their mouths from getting near the coral, so instead they begin to eat zooplankton—microscopic animals floating in the water.

SIBERIAN UNICORN

Hundreds of thousands of years ago, there was another type of one-horned animal. It could grow to six feet tall and fifteen feet long, and it lived in Siberia. It resembled the rhinoceros, but its horn was closer to its forehead. Most of these creatures died out about 350,000 years ago, but some survived for thousands of years more, as recently as 29,000 years ago, in a small area of Kazakhstan.

NARWHALS, *the* UNICORNS *of the* SEA

OF ALL the real-life creatures connected to unicorns, the narwhal is one of the most important.

Narwhals are whales that live in the Arctic Ocean, usually in small groups. Sometimes called a "sea unicorn," a male narwhal has a long, spiraling tusk. Their tusks can grow up to ten feet long. It's rare, but some females can grow a tusk, too.

These tusks are a type of canine tooth, similar to the pointed teeth that dogs, wolves, and humans have. But in narwhals, one tooth just keeps growing much longer than the others—so long that it pierces the narwhal's lip and becomes a tusk!

Narwhal tusks are full of nerves. They are covered with algae and sea lice, so they look green. Male narwhals sometimes cross their tusks as if they were sword fighting. But they don't hurt each other. They're usually much more careful than they would be in a real fight.

Sea lice are tiny, shrimp-like creatures that live on other sea animals.

WHAT ARE NARWHALS LIKE?
ASK *a* NARWHAL BIOLOGIST!

Kristin Laidre is an expert in narwhals. She's studied narwhals for more than fifteen years, and she's learned some amazing things about these mysterious creatures.

WHY NARWHALS HAVE TUSKS: "It's similar to the feathers of a peacock or the mane of a lion. It's a trait that lets males compete and females size up their mate."

WHAT'S INSIDE THEIR MOUTH: "Narwhals have no teeth. They only have that one tusk."

THEIR SPECIAL SKILLS: "They dive very deep, more than a mile below the sea surface. They take one deep breath. They make a half-hour-long dive. It's pretty extreme."

WHAT THEY FEEL LIKE: "They feel rubbery and a little bit like a wet, hard inner tube."

WHAT TO DO IF YOU SEE A NARWHAL: "Be very quiet, and don't move. They get scared easily and dive."

MEDIEVAL UNICORNS

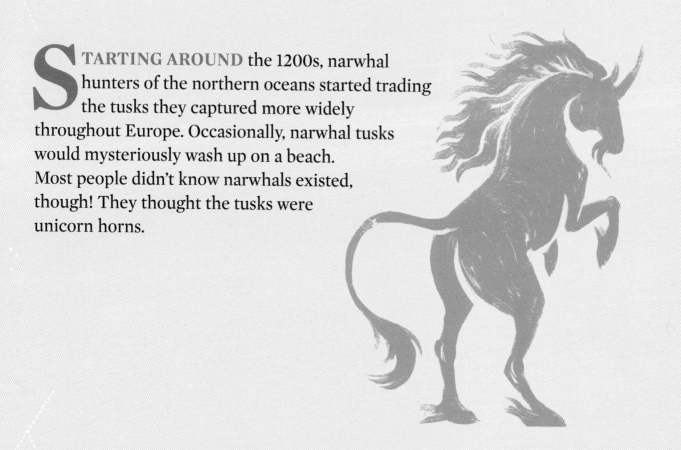

STARTING AROUND the 1200s, narwhal hunters of the northern oceans started trading the tusks they captured more widely throughout Europe. Occasionally, narwhal tusks would mysteriously wash up on a beach. Most people didn't know narwhals existed, though! They thought the tusks were unicorn horns.

Unicorns were incredibly popular in the medieval period (from the fifth through the fifteenth centuries). The religion of Christianity was becoming one of the most powerful forces in Europe, and Christian thinkers were trying to figure out what the stories in the Bible really meant. Over time, they started associating the unicorns mentioned in the Bible with Jesus Christ.

Like a unicorn, Christ was seen as being fierce and strong. Medieval artists started making paintings where unicorns were meant to represent Jesus. Once the image of unicorns became linked to Jesus, they started appearing everywhere.

the UNICORN TAPESTRIES

ONE OF the most famous examples of unicorns in medieval art is a set of seven tapestries made around the year 1500. They're known as *The Hunt of the Unicorn*, or the Unicorn Tapestries.

They're displayed in New York City in a museum called the Cloisters that was partly built using the stones and columns of medieval monasteries and convents from France and Spain.

To see the Unicorn Tapestries in New York, you walk through a French doorway carved from volcanic stone, with unicorns above it.

THERE'S A lot of mystery surrounding these seven tapestries. They may have been made as a wedding present, in a workshop in Belgium. But no one knows exactly where they were made or what their meaning is.

Most of them show hunters chasing a unicorn, in the same way people during the Middle Ages usually hunted deer. One tapestry, where a young woman helps tame the unicorn, is missing parts of the original. But it's clear from what we can see that with her help, the hunters capture and kill the unicorn.

One of the tapestries is different from the others, though. Here, the unicorn is alive but has been wounded. It has been captured behind a fence and is sitting among plants and flowers. This tapestry may have been created as a bedspread or canopy. It also may be meant to show that the unicorn has come back to life.

The Unicorn Tapestries are really big! They're twelve feet tall and anywhere from eight to fourteen feet wide. They take up the walls of an entire room, going from floor to ceiling. It would have taken a team of four to six weavers at least a year to make each one.

In the room where they hang, there's a surprise in the corner—an eight-foot-long narwhal tusk. The people who made these tapestries would have believed it actually came from a unicorn, and you can see that in their art. The unicorn's horn looks a lot like the narwhal tusk!

UNICORNS, LOVE,
and MARRIAGE

IN STORIES and art, young women and girls often helped capture unicorns, and this led to unicorns becoming a symbol of love in the Middle Ages. Many experts think that another famous set of medieval tapestries, called *The Lady and the Unicorn*, represents romantic love.

One of the first known unicorn-themed weddings was in 1468, for Margaret of York, the Duchess of Burgundy. She was the sister of the English king and was marrying a French duke. A set of narwhal tusks were hung over the table where the food was laid for the guests. And people wearing a unicorn costume came into the hall and circled the table!

Today, not much has changed. Unicorn-themed weddings are popular. And when a famous fashion designer created a unicorn wedding dress, he had two people in a giant white unicorn costume walk down the runway with the model.

What Does a Unicorn Wedding Dress Look Like?

It can have many layers of fabric, pastel rainbow colors, thousands of ribbons, glitter, lace, and even the image of a unicorn sewn across the front. But it is always a bit magical.

HOW *to* DEFEAT *a* UNICORN

IN THE Middle Ages, bestiary books, which were long records of all known animals, became popular. Many of them described unicorns and their natural enemies as if they were real.

HUNTERS

As the Unicorn Tapestries show, hunters were dangerous to unicorns. Unicorn meat was not supposed to be good to eat. But a unicorn horn was thought to have special powers. Like modern poachers, the hunter may have been after the horn, not the unicorn itself.

MAIDENS

Hunters were often aided by maidens—unmarried girls and young women. Medieval people believed that only maidens had the power to lure the unicorns close. As one nun explained in the twelfth century, the unicorn is surprised that the girls have no beards, like some hunters do. So the unicorn believes that the girls are friendly. But when the animal moves closer, the hunters sneak up and kill it.

ELEPHANTS

According to medieval bestiaries, elephants and unicorns were rivals who would attack each other. The unicorn's battle strategy: spear the elephant in the belly with its horn.

LIONS

Lions had a sneaky way of defeating unicorns. When a unicorn started to charge, the big cats would run toward a tree. The unicorn would run straight into the tree and get its horn stuck in the trunk. It wouldn't be able to move. Only then would the lion attack.

GREAT SCOT!
I SPY *a* UNICORN

BECAUSE **UNICORNS** were thought to be so powerful, aristocrats (wealthy or important people who were often friends of the king) started adopting them as symbols. Back in the twelfth century, the king of Scotland included a unicorn in his royal coat of arms. Soon, the unicorn became the national animal of Scotland! It's possible to find images of unicorns all over the country, even at the front of a Royal Navy ship called the HMS *Unicorn*.

One Scottish king in the fifteenth century had gold coins made with unicorns on them. They were worth eighteen shillings; a "half-unicorn" was worth nine shillings. (Today, that would be hundreds of dollars.)

The Scottish unicorn is sometimes shown with a golden chain, which may symbolize Scotland's strength. Since unicorns were almost impossible to catch, a king who could capture one and keep it chained up had to be pretty powerful.

The unicorn also happens to be an enemy of the lion. And lions are a symbol of England. Today, the two countries are united, but in the past when they were at war, it was fitting for the lion and unicorn banners to face off against each other.

WHY DO SOME UNICORNS HAVE WINGS?

IN THIRTEENTH- and fourteenth-century art, unicorns often have wings. But natural historians, like Ctesias and the writers who followed him, never mention wings at all. And all the animals that might have inspired unicorns live on the ground or in the ocean. So where did the idea come from?

One explanation is that artists thought of unicorns as monsters or, at the very least, made-up creatures. Other imaginary animals, like sphinxes and griffins, were often pictured with wings.

Naturally, artists eventually gave unicorns wings, too, as a way to signal how fanciful, fabulous, and fantastic they were.

What Is a Sphinx?

The mythical creature known as the sphinx has the head of a human and the body of a lion. The sphinx was thought to be very disloyal and untrustworthy.

What Is a Griffin?

The majestic and powerful griffin is a legendary creature with the head, wings, and talons of an eagle, and the body, tail, and legs of a lion. It is sometimes called the king of all creatures.

UNICORN HORNS *for* SALE!

AFTER NARWHAL tusks started showing up in Europe and being sold as unicorn horns, people were willing to pay incredible amounts of money to own one. By the 1500s, a unicorn horn was worth ten or twenty times its weight in gold. The king of France owned a horn that cost 17,000 ducats (hundreds of thousands of dollars in today's money)—quite a fortune.

Naturally, all sorts of royalty wanted unicorn horns of their own. Queen Elizabeth I of England was given a narwhal tusk she called the "Horn of Windsor."

The House of Habsburg, a family dynasty who ruled large parts of Europe for many centuries, had a narwhal tusk scepter.

The throne of Denmark, built in the 1600s, is made out of real narwhal tusks!

A scepter is a ceremonial staff used as a symbol of power, often by kings.

the SECRET POWER of UNICORN HORN

ONE OF the reasons "unicorn horns" were so expensive was that people believed that they had healing powers.

Because they believed a unicorn horn could protect you from poison, wealthy people would drop small bits into their drinks. Even wealthier people would have cups and knives made out of the actual horn. If the horn started to sweat, it was supposed to mean the food was poisoned.

For those who couldn't afford even a small piece of horn, there was also unicorn-horn powder. But the powder was usually just fossils, walrus tusks, or ordinary bones that had been ground into dust.

The belief in the power of unicorn horns lasted for centuries. In 1741, England still officially recognized it as a medicine.

HOW *to* TEST *a* UNICORN HORN

THE OWNERS of unicorn horns were often worried they had not been sold the real thing. (A reasonable worry since unicorns do not exist.) To find out if they had bought a "fake," they would test a horn's powers.

One simple test involved putting a piece of horn in water and watching to see if bubbles rose to the surface. Bubbles meant it was a genuine piece of unicorn horn. But that wasn't always considered reliable. Often the owners of unicorn horns would test them by feeding poison to a pigeon or chicken and then feeding it powdered unicorn horn. Somehow, some of the birds survived, making the test seem like a success and indicating that the horn was "real."

More rarely, the unicorn horn would even be tested on humans. Criminals sentenced to die would sometimes be forced to eat poison, followed by an antidote. (If it worked, they might be allowed to go free.)

Another test had its own dangers. A bit of the horn was put in a bowl or pot with three or four live scorpions and then covered. If the scorpions were dead after four hours, the horn was said to be the real deal.

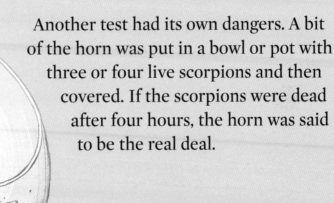

the *UNICORN* CURE

UNICORN HORN was believed to be such strong medicine that for many years, apothecaries stocked and sold it.

Over time, the unicorn came to be a symbol of an apothecary shop. The Society of Apothecaries in London adopted the unicorn as part of its coat of arms, and apothecary shops might have names like "Unicorn's Horn" or "Sign of the Unicorn." If you saw a unicorn sign above a shop, that would be a hint that you could buy medicine there.

An apothecary is a
person who prepares
and sells medicine.

the REAL PRICE of a HORN

ALTHOUGH AN international treaty has outlawed trade in rhinoceros horns, illegal markets still threaten the rhino population. Some people believe that ground rhinoceros-horn powder can treat fever, gout, headaches, vomiting, and hallucinations. And some families in Vietnam still buy pieces of rhino horn for a very sick person, to show they've done everything they possibly can to save them.

Like the powder once sold as "unicorn horn," rhino horn is incredibly expensive—more valuable than gold. At its peak price in 2012, rhino horn sold for around $30,000 per pound!

There's little scientific evidence to show that rhino-horn powder has any healing powers. But because the horns are so valuable, hunters and poachers have made the Indian rhinoceros vulnerable to extinction and African rhinos critically endangered. Where once there were hundreds of thousands of rhinoceroses, now there are only a few thousand left.

the UNICORN *in* *the* SKY

IN **1613,** a Dutch astronomer named Petrus Plancius proposed a new constellation, right between Canis Minor and Canis Major, the two dogs, and to the left of Orion. He named it Monoceros (remember the Greek term from page 9?)—the Unicorn.

Monoceros is one of the faintest constellations in the sky. It's difficult to see with the naked eye, but on a dark night, in a dark place, it just might be possible to find the elusive unicorn!

the TRUTH ABOUT UNICORNS

BY 1638, a Danish scientist named Ole Worm had found a narwhal tusk still attached to a narwhal skull. It was proof that "unicorn horns" weren't real. Ole spread the word around Europe that the horns belonged to a different (and equally wonderful) animal. But it took another century or so for most people to realize that they had been buying narwhal tusks all along.

Ole Worm, son of Willum Worm, was a natural history buff who often used a fancier, Latin version of his name: Olaus Wormius!

OLAUS WORMIUS

HOW COULD A UNICORN HORN GROW?
ASK *a* BIOLOGIST!

A TRUE horn is a bone surrounded by keratin, the material fingernails are made of. But horns don't start out as part of animals' skulls. They grow from "buds" in the skin and fuse to the skull later.

According to Brian Hall, a biologist who's an expert in bones, something would have to change before an animal was born for it to have only one horn. In a vertebrate (any animal with a spinal column), the left and right halves of the body develop separately, at first.

Soon, though, they come together to form central structures. The nose, for example, is a central structure. The heart is a central structure, with a left and right side.

But other features are paired—two eyes, two ears, two arms. One develops on each side of the body. Horns are supposed to be a paired structure. But if something goes wrong, they're not!

There are examples, for instance, of mutant cows with a single horn in the middle of their head. It all depends on something called the "hedgehog gene." If that genetic coding gets mixed up, the features that are supposed to show up on both sides of the body can merge into one.

So, if a two-horned animal had a malfunctioning hedgehog gene, its two horns *might* grow as one, instead.

a DEER BORN *with* ONE ANTLER

THE HEDGEHOG gene is more than just a theory.

In 2008, in a nature preserve in Italy, a very unusual roe deer was born. He had just one antler—right in the center of his head. Workers at the preserve named him Unicorn.

It's also possible for a deer to end up with just one antler if it hurts itself. A few years later, in 2014, another deer with one antler was found in Slovenia. Scientists believe that the Slovenia deer may have injured its antlers early in life, and they developed into one horn. But the Italian deer had not been injured. Most likely a variation in his genes—put in motion before he was born—was the reason he had just one antler.

the UNICORN SKELETON

OTTO VON GUERICKE

THE DISCOVERY of real, live narwhals did not stop Europeans from believing in unicorns. In the seventeenth century, one scientist reported proof of unicorns' existence—a full, real unicorn skeleton.

In 1663, miners in Germany were working in a cave when they came upon a set of large, unusual bones. Otto von Guericke, a local scientist, saw the bones and later described them in one of his books.

"It was resting on its hindquarters," he wrote, "as animals are wont to do, with its head reared back." The key part of the skeleton, though, was the horn, which von Guericke said was as thick as a man's arm. His account was convincing enough that another natural history book, called *Protogaea*, included a drawing of the same "unicorn skeleton" in 1749.

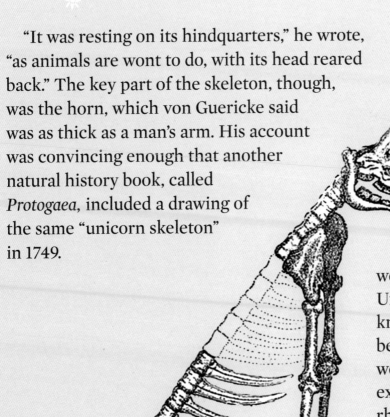

The cave where these bones were found is still called the Unicorn Cave. But today we know that the bones didn't belong to a unicorn at all. They were a group of fossils from extinct mammoths and woolly rhinoceroses that had gotten all jumbled up.

STEP RIGHT UP, SEE *the* UNICORN!

HIMALAYAN SHEEP

In 1906, a strange herd of sheep came to live at the London Zoological Gardens. They had been a gift from Nepal to the Prince of Wales, the future King George V, when he toured British India.

Sheep usually have two horns, but some of these had three or four. Two of the sheep, though, had only one horn—they were called unicorn sheep.

British writers reported that these were a very special breed of sheep, until a British representative in Nepal learned the truth.

When the sheep were very young and their horns had begun to grow, the herder would brand their horn buds with an iron, damaging them. That made the two horns grow into just one, right in the middle of the sheep's skulls.

DOVE'S UNICORN BULL

An American scientist, Franklin Dove, used a similar technique to create a unicorn bull in the 1930s. He performed surgery on the calf, removed its horn buds from their original location, and replaced them closer together. When they grew in, they formed one single horn.

LANCELOT, *the* LIVING UNICORN

THE MOST famous man-made unicorn joined the circus. In 1985, the Ringling Bros. and Barnum & Bailey circus started claiming that its show included the "Living Unicorn." His name was Lancelot.

For a unicorn, Lancelot was small, just about two and a half feet tall. Like some of the unicorns described hundreds of years earlier, he was about the size of a goat and had a goat's beard. In fact, except for his horn, he looked a lot like a regular old goat.

The horn was real! The circus allowed an X-ray to be taken of Lancelot in order to prove it. Reporters got their proof, but Lancelot hadn't been born that way.

Lancelot started life as an ordinary goat. But his owner, a man named Oberon Zell, had been experimenting with turning goats into unicorns. Using a technique similar to Dove's, he encouraged the goats' horns to grow together until he had a flock of one-horned goats. Lancelot joined the circus for a few years, but the others lived happily on Zell's California farm.

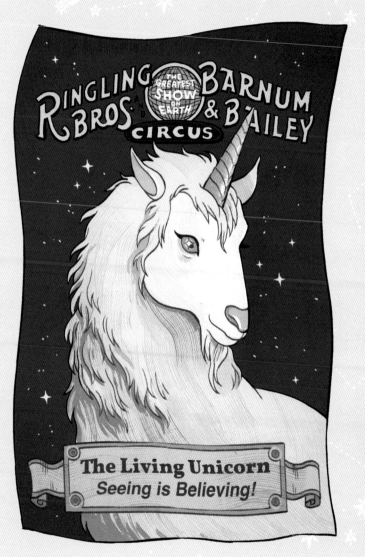

HUMANS CAN BE UNICORNS, TOO

IT'S ALSO possible for humans to grow horns, of a sort. These horns start with a skin lesion and are made from the same material as fingernails and rhinoceros horns.

Usually these horns are very, very small bumps. But sometimes the horns can grow close to a foot long. And sometimes they grow on people's heads.

It's rare for anyone to grow a horn, and there are only a handful of cases in the past few hundred years where the horns have grown large enough for others to see.

They're not very common, and they can be painful. But they *are* real.

UNICORN FANTASIES

PEOPLE REPORTED unicorn sightings for a surprisingly long time. As late as the 1790s, at least one writer still thought there could be unicorns in South Africa. This was after the creation of the United States, the French Revolution, and the European discovery of Australia.

Most people eventually realized that unicorns were made-up creatures, and they started writing about them in fiction and fantasy books instead of natural history books.

In the early 1800s, the Brothers Grimm included a unicorn in one of their fairy tales, "The Brave Little Tailor." After a king orders him to capture a unicorn, the tailor adopts the age-old strategy used by lions— he quickly steps aside and lets the unicorn ram its horn into a tree.

By the time unicorns first appeared in a Disney movie called *Fantasia*, they were small and good-natured. They seemed like they might be fun to play with.

In 1941, a book called *The Colt from Moon Mountain*, by Dorothy Lathrop, told the story of a girl who befriends a young white unicorn in the forest near her house. Thirty years later, the story inspired one of the most famous fantasy books about unicorns—*The Last Unicorn*, by Peter S. Beagle.

By the second half of the twentieth century, unicorns had taken the form that we know today—white, majestic, gentle, horse-like creatures with magical powers.

UNICORN MAGIC

ONCE UNICORNS had moved completely into the realm of fantasy, they gained all sorts of new powers. Authors and filmmakers gave them special talents.

In *The Last Unicorn*, the unicorn's horn has healing powers, and in the Harry Potter books, drinking unicorn's blood can keep someone from dying. In other books and movies, unicorns often have the ability to communicate telepathically (they can read minds!), extra strength, speed, or intelligence, and they can even perform magic.

a SPECIAL HORSE . . .
WITHOUT *a* HORN

MOST OFTEN, fantasy unicorns are pure white. But even when you're not looking for a unicorn, it's rare to find a pure white horse.

For a horse to be pure white, it needs to have white hair and colorless skin. These traits are passed from parents to offspring. In order for a horse to be entirely white, it must have at least one all-white parent.

As common as unicorn stories are around the world, stories about white horses are even more so. In many myths, the hero rides a white horse—no horn necessary. In Greek mythology, the famous flying horse Pegasus is white, and in Indian mythology, the god Vishnu rides a white horse to save the world.

Pegasus is the mythical winged stallion of Greek mythology. He is the son of Poseidon and Medusa.

the BEST WAY *to* HUNT *a* UNICORN

IN 1971, Lake Superior State University in Michigan formed a group of unicorn hunters.

These devoted unicorn hunters had many rituals. They started traditions like burning snowmen in honor of spring and hosting a tournament for stone skipping. They would also select words they would like to banish from the English language. But their main purpose was to try to find unicorns.

During Unicorn Questing Season, hunters have to follow certain rules. They can only hunt one unicorn each month, using poetry, a serious sense of purpose, and sweet talk. And they can only target male unicorns.

The Unicorn Hunters advise bringing along a small bottle of Unicorn Lure, a pair of hoof trimmers, and a curry comb for grooming.

Unicorn Questing Season lasts all year except for one day—St. Agnes' Eve, January 20.

For anyone interested in unicorn hunting, Lake Superior State University offers licenses on its website. They are valid on Earth, unexplored areas of the moon, throughout the Milky Way, and anywhere else unicorns might be found.

the 1980s:
UNICORN POWER DECADE

IN THE 1980s, images of unicorns in many popular formats began to sell in large numbers. Unicorns were suddenly everywhere.

- One of the first characters artist Lisa Frank drew was a happy-go-lucky unicorn with a rainbow mane that appeared on her stickers, folders, and other products. The unicorn is named Markie, after one of Lisa's friends.

- My Little Pony was invented, and in the second year they were sold, some of the ponies were unicorns, with spiral horns, glittery symbols, and a streak of special color in their hair. (Unicorn ponies are also called Alicorns!)

- *The Last Unicorn* was turned into an animated movie.

- A book called *Whisper the Winged Unicorn* told the story of a unicorn who lived in Rainbow Forest. It came with stickers inside. (Unicorn stickers were very popular!)

- The cartoon hero She-Ra, Princess of Power, rode a unicorn with multicolored wings.

- In the movie *Blade Runner,* an important dream sequence had a white unicorn in it.

- Another famous movie called *Legend* featured two white unicorns who are captured by goblins.

- Lancelot the goat unicorn made his first appearance in Ringling Bros. and Barnum & Bailey circus.

RAINBOWS *and* UNICORNS

UNICORNS AND rainbows, rainbows and unicorns: These days, a unicorn might have a rainbow mane, or a rainbow bursting out of the clouds behind her, or a rainbow path to walk on. But this association is relatively new.

In the 1970s, rainbow-patterned everything had taken over stores. Then, as unicorns became less and less rare, they started appearing alongside rainbows.

Unicorns had been accepted as magical creatures, and rainbows have their own built-in magic. So this seemed like a perfectly natural pairing.

Once united, though, unicorns and rainbows became inseparable. And rainbows are now the unofficial color scheme of unicorns everywhere.

UNICORN FOODS

IT'S HARD to say exactly when people started connecting rainbow-colored food with unicorns. But what's known for sure is that in 2016, a café in New York City started making Unicorn Lattes.

They were a beautiful bright blue, with rainbow sprinkles on top. The lattes were flavored with ginger, lemon, and vanilla.

The next year, Starbucks created a "Unicorn Frappuccino," a purple, mango cream drink that changed to bright pink when stirred!

Here are some other unicorn foods that might be found in the wild.

UNICORN CUPCAKES: Common. Often display rainbow-colored icing, sometimes have a candy horn.

UNICORN FROOT LOOPS: Rare. Red, blue, and purple cereal with "magic cupcake" flavor.

UNICORN SMOOTHIE BOWL: Restricted habitat. Bright pink, swirled with blue, sprinkled with fruit. Found most often in fancy, health-conscious cafés.

UNICORN HOT CHOCOLATE: Common. Pink or blue, characterized by abundant sprinkles on top of whipped cream.

UNICORN ELOTE: Very rare. Grilled corn, covered either in dyed mayonnaise or colored chocolate. More monster than magic.

UNICORN TOAST: Restricted habitat. Made with colored cream cheese, swirled in stripes. Natural dyes only, please! A DIY favorite.

SECRET UNICORN
INGREDIENTS

WHAT GIVES unicorn food its color? Sometimes, it's just food coloring. But sometimes it's very special, sparkly ingredients. They can be as hard to find as a unicorn itself!

The creator of unicorn toast used freeze-dried strawberry powder to create pink cream cheese, and drops of chlorophyll to create green cream cheese!

Unicorn bowls often include pitaya, or dragon fruit, which comes from a cactus, to create a bright pink color.

The blue of the Unicorn Latte comes from spirulina, an edible algae.

UNICORN POOP

AT SOME point, the relationship between rainbows and unicorns became so close, people started saying that unicorns poop out rainbows. Often, this is represented in cookies, candy, and other sweet treats.

A RECIPE FOR UNICORN POOP BARK

You'll need:

- 5 cups candy coating (choose at least three different colors) OR 5 cups white chocolate chips and some food coloring
- At least two fun toppings: rainbow sprinkles, candy pearls, mini-marshmallows, edible glitter, or other small and colorful candy
- Waxed paper

1. Place each color of candy coating in a separate bowl. (If you're using white chocolate, divide it up into 3–5 bowls.)

2. Melt the candy in the microwave. (Follow the directions on the package!)

3. If using white chocolate chips, add a few drops of coloring to the bowls to create blue, pink, purple, or yellow candy, then melt. It's okay to leave one bowl white, too.

4. Put a sheet of waxed paper on a baking sheet.

5. Pour the candy onto the paper, making small circles of different colors that overlap or blend together.

6. Use a knife or a toothpick to create swirls of color.

7. Sprinkle the toppings all over the candy.

8. Put the baking sheet in the refrigerator for 30 minutes, or until the candy has hardened.

Break into pieces and enjoy your UNICORN POOP BARK!

TWENTY-FIRST-CENTURY UNICORNS

UNICORNS MAY not be found in the wild, but they can easily be found online. When videos were first becoming popular on the Internet, one early star was Charlie the Unicorn, a gray and grumpy unicorn whose friends keep getting him into trouble.

In the game *Robot Unicorn Attack*, a unicorn runs across the screen and has to jump across pits and smash into stars to survive.

There's also a unicorn emoji! You might use it when you're excited about something special or unique, or if someone is trying to convince you that something fake is actually real.

And there are plenty of unicorn memes. One famous image shows a cat standing on top of a unicorn, saying "Welcome to the Internet, Please Follow Me."

The word *unicorn* also now has a second meaning—a startup business (a new company) that's valued at more than $1 billion. These are very rare, but unlike actual unicorns, they *do* exist.

WHAT'S *a* UNICORN HORN MADE OF?

IT'S EASY enough to buy a unicorn horn—at a craft store or online. In 2017, a store specializing in unicorn horns opened in Brooklyn, New York. Horns are available in gold, glitter, or almost any imaginable color, in sizes that range from short and stubby to majestically long. These unicorn horns are made not from bone but from ribbon, thread, felt, fabric, elastic, and stuffing. If you want to make your own, you can also use Styrofoam, clay, paper, or even your own hair, twisted around a cone. Try it!

How does it stay on? Many unicorn horns for people can be worn like headbands. They're made for horses, too, so your favorite pony can transform into a more magical being.

WHERE *to* FIND UNICORNS

The story of unicorns isn't over. For thousands of years, these creatures have been evolving, as human imaginations change them. They may not be real, but they're a powerful idea. Today, it's easier than ever to find a unicorn. Just look for them. They're everywhere!

Monoceros constellation
The night sky

Unicorn Tapestries
New York, NY, USA

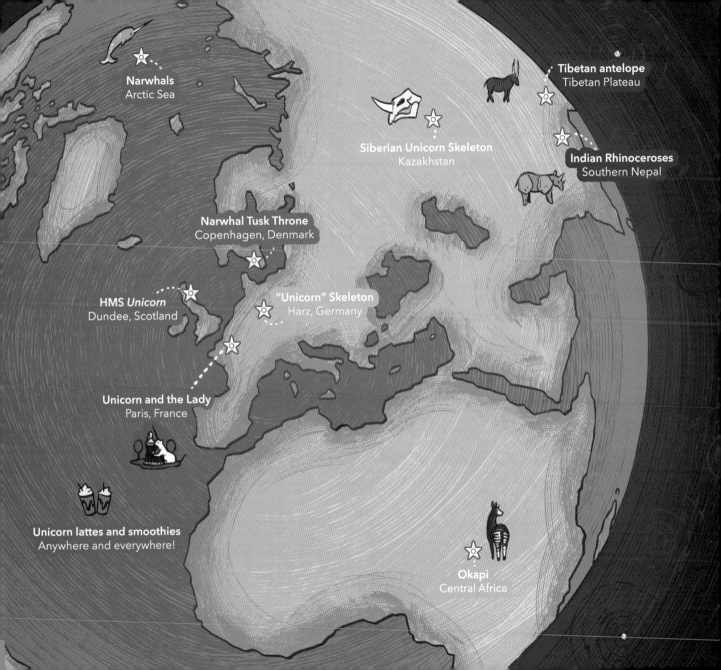

Narwhals
Arctic Sea

Tibetan antelope
Tibetan Plateau

Siberian Unicorn Skeleton
Kazakhstan

Indian Rhinoceroses
Southern Nepal

Narwhal Tusk Throne
Copenhagen, Denmark

HMS *Unicorn*
Dundee, Scotland

"Unicorn" Skeleton
Harz, Germany

Unicorn and the Lady
Paris, France

Unicorn lattes and smoothies
Anywhere and everywhere!

Okapi
Central Africa

BIBLIOGRAPHY

*Books for young readers

*Beagle, Peter S. *The Last Unicorn*. San Diego: IDW Publishing, 2011. (Graphic novel adaptation by Peter B. Gillis, and illustrated by Renae De Liz with colors by Ray Dillon.)

Ettinghausen, Richard. *The Unicorn: Studies in Muslim Iconography*. Washington, DC: Smithsonian Institution, 1950.

Freeman, Margaret B. *The Unicorn Tapestries*. New York: Metropolitan Museum of Art, 1976.

Gotfredsen, Lise. *The Unicorn*. New York: Abbeville Press, 1999.

Lavers, Chris. *The Natural History of Unicorns*. New York: HarperCollins, 2009.

*Leaf, Christina. *Extremely Weird Animals: Narwhal*. Minnetonka, MN: Pilot Books, 2014.

*Poltarnees, Welleran. *A Book of Unicorns*. San Diego: Green Tiger Press, 1978.

Shepard, Odell. *The Lore of the Unicorn*. New York: Dover Publications, 1993. (Originally published 1930.)